GOD LIGHTS HIS CANDLES

Poems

Dorothy E. Morris

Introduction by
Sam Cornish,
Boston Poet Laureate

Dorothy E Morris

Previously published in the *South Boston Literary Gazette*:
"After the Storm," "All Hallows Eve," "Cabin Fever," "Canon in D," "Gale Winds:
Stolen Kisses"

Previously published in *Celebrating Poets over 70*: "Memories"

ISBN 978-0-9846614-2-8

Designed by
FLAR Design
Allston, MA 02134

Proofreading assistance by Jim P. McDevitt and Kathryn L. Carroll

Published by
Ibbetson Street Press
25 School Street
Somerville, MA 02143
617-628-2313

9 8 7 6 5 4 3 2 1
First Edition

TO MY SIBLINGS

Mano a mano
Corazón a corazón

CONTENTS

INTRODUCTION

Dorothy Morris reveals herself to us through her love of nature and portraits of family and people observed through her walks on Boston's Castle Island and other local landscapes:

> After three straight days
> Of unyielding snow,
> I joyfully travel to
> My favorite island
> To enjoy nature.

The poems in *God Lights His Candles* are about spiritual longing in the language of a poet who has read Dickinson, Poe, Yeats and Whitman, as well as Mary Oliver and other contemporaries. Although Morris has lived most of her life in the Boston area, she has traveled widely abroad, and uses that experience to shape her poems.

Dorothy Morris is a poet of the interior, the innermost self; her life experiences are reborn and revisited in her poems. One of the pleasures of this collection is in seeking out the influences from her life experience. With confessional poets such as Sylvia Plath, the poet's life is laid bare on the page. Morris is more private, even though the truth is there beneath the lyric line and the familiar phrase. In this respect, her poems are postcards in communication between the reader and the poet who is discovering her craft.

The book opens with "Spring 2009":

> The world is fresh and new.
> Overnight spring has burst through
> Like a rainbow.

suggesting a spiritual awakening and concluding with the symbolic rainbow, as if a period of trouble has passed and the poet's life has entered a new world, as if a door has opened.

Throughout this volume the poems shift from darkness to light as the fog lifts. The title poem, "God Lights His Candles," with its oblique reference to Yeats' "The Ballad of Moll Magee," also speaks to the poet's relationship to the poem itself as well as to the natural world and a lifetime of reading. Her book is joyful; a spiritual odyssey, concluding with these lines from the ringing of the bells:

> And when my traveling is done,
> I will hear the ringing of the bells.

The poet has discovered herself beyond endings or goodbyes,

rising above sentiment and fear of death. From the comforts of faith to the acceptance of memory, the spirit that one experiences lives as the poems in some deep secure self in the creative spirit of the artist. From "Down the Cawdor Trail — Scotland":

> Dark these woods.
> I am not alone.

Emily Dickinson was able to live fully within herself and find a universe there to explore and travel. Similarly, Dorothy Morris finds this universe through walks and meditations on the land and ocean, and her poetry grows out of this inspiration:

> Do not disturb:
> The bees are intoxicated
> With the perfumed air.

Unlike the student using the voices of other poets and writing to assignment, Morris displays a constant effort to discover the truth about what is seen, felt and experienced. Dorothy Morris is her own teacher and influence, and this is the poet's journey. Her collection is both moving and enlightening.

— Sam Cornish

Arboretum in May

SPRING 2009

The world is fresh and new.
Overnight spring has burst through
Like a rainbow.

Once dead trees are heavy with
Blossoms.
Burdened by abundance, each branch
Bears itself.

Snowdrops the harbinger,
But each young tulip now receives
The new rain with thirsty lip.

Trembling in the warm breeze
The cherry tree exudes its perfume.
Its gaiety a light to the welcoming dawn.

Jubilant, Jeune, Joyful.

ARBORETUM IN MAY

Strolling down the walk
Between two rows of lilac blooms
I tuck my nose into the fragrant blossoms,
Let the sweetness intoxicate me
Like a glass of pinot grigio.

White, lilac, of course, even blue.
A tiny tree named Tinkerbell.
And a huge late-blooming tree
Seed brought from Japan.

At a pool
A blue heron pauses on one foot.

The winds blow, the blossoms fall.

SPRING: BEACH WALK

In early spring
Along the seawall

The sun is playing
Hide and seek

With shadows.
Black and white,

Dark and light,
Salt and pepper,

Yin and yang.
Gu/ru...

Out of darkness
Night to light

Traversing the way

In search of
Eternal grace.

SUNSET: ORMOND BEACH

In the west, over the Intercoastal Waterway,
The sun goes down in flames
While here, in the East,
At the edge of the Atlantic,
In a pyrotechnic reflection
I see, as from my first view
From a 747,
The high peaks and spires of the pink- and white-topped Alps
On a late-night
Transatlantic flight to Europe.

JULY BENEDICTION

Twilight.
The sails are coming down.
Sun is waning.
Serenity.

The senior couples
Side by side on benches
Gazing out to sea —

Fourth of July

FOURTH OF JULY

For my grandnephew

You rock!
Forget Woodstock —
I wasn't there.
It's two thousand eight
And I'm rocking to
James Taylor's band
On my feet
Swaying to "Sweet Baby James."
Singing
Like I used
To do to you,
Little baby James.

NARCISSUS AT THE POOL

He struts along the water's edge
And preens himself — so cool.

Bewitched by his image
At the corner of my pool.

His kingly image charms,
His gifts he starts to ply.

Narcissus at the pool,
Or a monarch butterfly?

IMAGES

-1-

On a looping wire
Myriad starlings squat
Like black Majorca pearls.

-2-

The black hooded ducks
Glide smoothly in file
As if to chapel.

-3-

It's been three years.
I saw a crimson cardinal.
Was it you?

THE BERKSHIRES

Hills, hills, hills
And below, the slim white birch among the pines
Invokes the ancient gods where
Other feet have trod.
Other eyes of stealthy, silent men —
Brave, strong women were here
Pagans, they say.

The hills hold peaks and valleys
Like the journey of my life.
Men want to reach the peaks,
The challenge calls them
But the valleys tell us
Something too.

TAKING TIME...
OCTOBER EVENING AT JENSEN'S

"I lift up my eyes to the hills."

The valley spreads out below
Dotted with color,
Not yet peak.

The yellow begonias,
The drone of the bumble bees.

The mutt comes out
And swallows one.

The far off call of a bird,
The hum of telephone wires,

And the negligible sound of
Distant traffic.

A monarch butterfly arcs high,
And below him a small yellow
Traces the grooves of the new-mown lawn.

Below, the birch trees' limbs
Unfold like cobwebs' veins.

Chickadees sit on a dead tree.
I ask the old man
"Why don't you chop it down?"

"Because the birds sit in it...
And I want to see the birds."

ELEGY

"At five o'clock in the afternoon." *

It's a lonely swim at the pool.
The sun has disappeared,
And as I surface,
A chill.

Was it only the fear of ice
Or the cold to come
That brought sudden despair?
Or something deeper,
A long-gone September
When summer ended,
Bringing regret, guilt or grief.

And what of growing old?

Will all my days be filled with regret
Or will happier memories grace those days?

* from "Lament for Ignacio Sanchez Mejios"
by Federico Garcia Lorca

Changeling

ADVENT 2007

The Mormon Temple Choir is singing
Magnificat.
I catch some of the Latin words,
How could I not,
After so many childhood Latin masses.

In my car mirror I watch the sun
Reflecting on the water of the bay.
I think: grace.
How one might dip one's fingers
In the water
Or naked, immerse oneself
In the icy pool
To be clean.

But grace is not
To be held and touched, smelt or tasted.
It is ephemeral, like quicksilver
Or the sudden glimpse of a hummingbird
On the wing.

Yes, here we are in time,
And we must be patient.
Watch carefully in awe
For a silent glimpse of grace.
And to praise Him; praise Him.

AFTER THE STORM:
WINTER 2007-2008

-1-

As a child, I called them fairy trees
Those icy, glistening gems
In the dead of winter.

After the storm
In the forest on either side
The tall slim trees
Covered with ice
Hard as diamonds,
As bright as light.
But brittle, too,
Like the heart.

-2-

A Nor'easter came through.
The trees are
Transformed,
Laden with mounds
Of snow
All now Christmas trees.
As pure and new
As if there were no war,
No famine.
Perfect.
Fresh, newly formed, as if
From the hand of God.

-3-

Why do they call it
The Dead of Winter?
When the tiniest blade
Brings promise,
And one can and must hope.

CABIN FEVER

After three straight days
Of unyielding snow,
I joyfully travel to
My favorite island
To enjoy nature.

But the island is ice-locked.
Only a squirrel and I
Enjoy the scene.

Here the snow is still white;
Quiet and beauty reign.
A cold and austere sun
Sheds its light
Over clouds that recall
The White Mountains.

It is a day that skiers love,
And I travel back in time
To a Franconia
Of lost youth on open
Slopes and wooded trails,
Of joy in flying over snow
Or conquering a mogul.

Of twilight
By a fireside
Warmed by a hot drink
And après ski sharing.
Of exploits related
Mishaps laughingly shared,
Banked desires,
And wishful bravado
Under the mountains of white.
Long ago,
When winters always
Promised spring.

THE WIND AND THE SEA

Like a dipping wing of a monarch butterfly,
The yellow-spotted sail loses ground
And falls toward the sea.

The wind surfer valiantly holds on
Trying to steady the sail in the choppy sea.
He struggles, man against nature,
And finally, abetted by the wind,
He rises, the wind at his back,
Triumphant at last.

MAELSTROM

They come on like gangbusters,
Flocks of black birds,
Undercoating of white wings,
Out of control.
If they have a leader,
I can't discern it.
Swooping, darting, dipping,
Diving, rising in unison,
Tossed about as in a storm.

THE FOG

The fog rushed in,
Along the causeway,
And enveloped us from both sides.

Shut out the airplanes,
But not their noise,
Dogs barked
But were not seen,
Through the mist,
The seagulls were still visible.

The causeway was now an island.
Disembodied voices could be heard,
And I was confused.

A man approached in the fog.
A British voice announced,
"At least I can see my feet.

"In London's last great fog," he said,
"The burning coal mixed with the fog
And caused 500 elderly deaths."

As we parted ways,
I heard him call,
"Watch out for Jack the Ripper."

I shivered.

CHANGELING

I've known your many moods
Your rising and falling —
Your tempest, your rage —
Your thunderous roar
Your passion and your chill.

But today
With the sun shining on you,
You seem almost serene,
Tranquil, gentle
As with a sigh
You glide gracefully to shore.

GALE WINDS: STOLEN KISSES

Leaving their car,
The wind nearly knocked them over.
They were not young,
Both gray-haired, plain,
Her wedding band had worn a groove
On her finger.
She wore a windbreaker,
But the wind tore against the hood.
Her husband carefully covered her head.
As the wind continued to blow,
He tied the hood.
Face to face they smiled.
I thought, "Now she will kiss him."
But no, they exchanged a word
Then started their walk.

GALE WINDS #2: THE BALLET

As the wind whipped a froth on the bay,
It blew a solitary kite surfer.
Carried aloft,
He executed a graceful pirouette
High in the air
As the crowd breathed.

Other surfers joined him.
Their brothers pumped air
And worried their kites.
Barefoot, black clad,
Their chariots of blue,
Black, yellow, red
Bore them ever higher.

The leader held on
With one hand
Orchestrating his dance
To the music in the wind
Or within.

His kite rose — a daring height
Only to fall like Icarus
To the water.
A troop of gallants,
Replacements waiting on the beach
Until the surfer rises ever higher,
A graceful pirouette; his ballet
A rebuke to the earthbound.

WINTER TWILIGHT: WOLLASTON BEACH

Last pink ribbons on the horizon.
A full moon, cold and serene
Lights the snow-covered sand
As a distant star,
Minot Light,
Blends its rays
With the beams of car lights.

But this moon is not constant,
Moving ahead of me and
Playing hide and seek
With the clouds

As I, head tucked down
Against the winter wind,
Hide from the fierce cold.

DECEMBER BLIZZARD

At twilight,
God lights His candles
With flame
And throws down fire
To ignite the sky.

Red against
The pure white earth below.

Memories

MEMORIES

Strange how memories can maim or
Sustain us.
Consider the pear tree —
Its white blossoms
Waving kisses at me every spring
In my fourth floor aerie,
Causing poetry to spring unbounded
From some deep well of forgetfulness.

Though gone now,
It can still bring forth a resurrection
Every spring,
And yet unlock
The despairing fruit of buried memory.

CANON IN D

When I was young,
How I used to rant,
While washing dishes.

Now in the soapy waters
I find therapy
For heart and hand.

Soaking in the suds,
Listening to the joyous sound of
"Canon in D." *

* Johann Pachelbel (1653 – 1706)

PILLOW TALK

When we were little girls
We shared a double bed,
And whispered our secrets
In heart-to-heart talks.

When I was twelve,
You said you would be a nun.
I went to sleep in tears
That you would leave me.

Now here we are again
Together in our later years
Sharing a room at night
For a brief respite.

We've had a few laughs
And a few tears,
And now I lie awake
While you sleep.

Sleepless,
I listen to your soft breathing,
And time my breaths
To align with yours.

In A Scottish Garden

IN A SCOTTISH GARDEN
(Crathes Castle, Banchory, Scotland)

Do not disturb:
The bees are intoxicated
With the perfumed air.
A white butterfly
Is a gentler emissary.

And here the masterpiece,
Lady Burnett's pool garden.
Assuredly a pool,
Replete with pond lilies.

Oranges and yellows
Dazzle,
And below…
Late bloomers — red roses
As red as Scottish blood
On the tranquil soil.

Do not disturb.

DOWN THE CAWDOR TRAIL —
SCOTLAND

Dark these woods.
I am not alone.

For company,
The murmuring brook.
And a hasty bird
Has left a gray feather,
A signature;
Here a lonely pinecone
From a living tree,
And the scent of
Wild raspberries.

Nearby a stone bench
Invites a pause.

And as I descend
Deeper and deeper,
Growth and darkness
Overtake me until
I barely see the way.

I am not alone.
For at my back
I feel the breath of
Duncan, Banquo and the Laird.

MACHU PICCHU

Finally, we've arrived at this sacred place.
Up the hairpin curves dropping off into Limbo
To the hallowed stones above where millions
Of barefoot feet have trod
Over the weathered, grooved rocks.

Here at the top of the mud-covered treeless montañas
One could step off into the clouds
And touch the tip of heaven.

And what of this giant culture
These proud people of five centuries past
And the mystery of where they have gone?

Perhaps the answer lies only in the large black,
Wondering eyes of the niños
Or the wizened, grooved faces of los viejos.

RONDA AFTER THE RAIN

The yellow flowers glitter against the velvet grass
The white almond blossoms waft gently in the breeze
The orange fruit falls quietly to the ground.
While the sun illuminates the deep valley
And above, the snows birth a waterfall down the steep slopes.
Then the clouds enter in and darkness falls again.

THE ORANGES OF SEVILLE

For Marie

The oranges of Seville are bitter, they say.
Fit only for marmalade, the Spaniards say.

"Mi amiga está enferma.
"Señor, la sopa para mi amiga, por favor."

In the gardens of the Reales Alcázar
The orange trees glow,

Their fruit lies rotting on the ground.
"Mi amiga está muerta."

I bit into an orange from Seville today.
The oranges of Seville are bitter, they say.

Blessings

BLESSING

"The Lord bless you and keep you.
May He make His face to shine upon you."

A toddler turned and faced the congregation.
A wide smile graced his face,
Shining like the Christmas candle
And lighting the faces
Of the elderly women before him.

MARY'S MASS

The priest takes the Host
And breaks it in two.
He holds the fragment in his hands.
A child cries.
And in the ringing of the bells,
My heart fractures.

EUCHARIST

I hold the Host
Making a cup.
Like Mother Mary
I lift Him up.

I take the Host
And sup
Then drink from
The Blessing Cup.

Oh, moment sublime
When mortal meets Divine.

HOLY THURSDAY

High noon at the Great Meadow
On the cusp of the Concord River
Within the tangled trees and weeds
Two kayakers glide.

A muskrat builds his dam
And a lone Canada goose
Poses on one leg.
Guarding the gander
Resting in the weeds
On her egg.

At evening Mass,
A distraction in the pew,
Heads turn as a chubby pre-toddler
Coos cheerfully.

In the pew before us
A small blonde woman in a loose blouse
Prays.
Her husband turns to look at her
Then gently, reverently pats her belly.

New spring.
New life.

In Church

Down the aisle
Comes a very old man,
Gnarled, bald, stooped,
A little girl by the hand.
So small and fragile.
They find the pew;
He ushers her in.

All through the Mass
His eye never wavers.
His right arm is there
To guide and protect.

She stands on the kneeler
On tiptoe to see.
Alert and studious.

Then, wearying of the mysteries
She puts thumb to mouth
And snuggles into the crook
Of that still strong arm.

Little ship going out
Into a stormy sea,
Steady as she goes.
She will need that strong arm.

ALL HALLOW'S EVE

I spied a three-year-old on his bicycle
His mother following with a baby carriage.
The boy stopped, hopped off his bicycle,
And with one hand pulled up two dandelions.

"For you, Mom," he said proudly.
She laughed, "Two weeds."
"Lucky you," I called to her.

Sometimes I wonder if God is three years old.

RINGING OF THE BELLS

The cherry trees lower their heads
Under the burden of blossoms.
As from the Gothic towers of St. Agatha,
I hear the ringing of the bells.

It was at a small parish church in Quebec
That I first heard the ringing of the bells
When I was twenty-two.

From Crane's bell rope to
The rope swinger of Notre Dame
At Angelus, I have heard the bells ring.

From the train window, as I spied
The spires of the Queen's jewel at Chartres,
I heard the ringing of the bells.

At a postwar St. Paul's,
Where a blade of grass grew in the ruins
And where the warriors slept in peace
I heard the bells ring.

Up and down the length of Italy,
From Francis' church at walled Assisi,
To the zebra'd face of Siena's cathedral,

From the campanile at Firenze,
To the many towers of San Gimignano,
The bells rang out.

And when my traveling is done,
I will hear the ringing of the bells.